The Nature Kid's Guide to
BUGS

DAVID ANDERSON

LP Media Inc. Publishing
Text copyright © 2026 by LP Media Inc.
All rights reserved.

For information address LP Media Inc. Publishing,
30012 Variolite St NW, Princeton MN 55371
www.lpmedia.org

Publication Data

Bugs
The Nature Kid's Guide to Bugs — First edition.

Summary: "Learn all about Bugs, the Nature Kid Way"
— Provided by publisher.

ISBN: 979-8-89818-189-5

[1. Bugs – Non-Fiction] I. Title.

Title: The Nature Kid's Guide to Bugs

CONTENTS

BUG BONANZA

Scientists have named over one million kinds of insects, but millions more are still waiting to be discovered!

Buzz! A small winged creature zips right past your nose.

Bugs are everywhere! They crawl under rocks, fly through the air, and swim in ponds. There are more bugs on Earth than any other kind of animal. In fact, scientists think there are over 10 million different species!

Most people use the word "bug" for any small creature with lots of legs. In this book, we do too! You will meet beetles, ants, butterflies, and many more amazing critters.

Some bugs are big enough to cover your hand. Others are so tiny you can barely see them. Some look like leaves, sticks, or even flowers. Get ready to explore the wild, wonderful world of bugs!

BUG BODIES

A dragonfly has about 30,000 tiny lenses in each eye, letting it see all around it at once!

Crunch! An ant snaps its jaws and picks up a big seed.

All insects have three main body parts. They have a head, a middle part, and a back end. They also have six legs and two feelers called antennae on their heads.

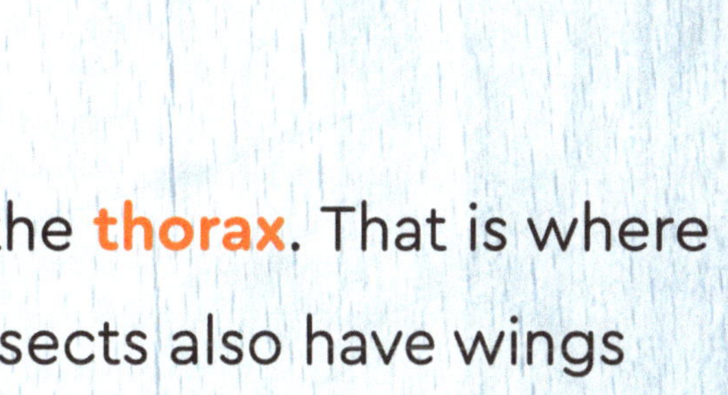

The middle part is called the **thorax**. That is where the legs connect. Many insects also have wings attached here.

Insects do not have bones inside like we do. Instead, they wear their skeleton on the outside! This hard shell protects their soft insides and keeps them safe from harm.

BUG POWER

Dung beetles use the Milky Way galaxy to navigate at night—they are the only insects known to steer by starlight.

Push! A Dung Beetle pushes a ball of poop across the desert.

Bugs have amazing powers! Some are super strong. A dung beetle can push a ball of dung over 1,000 times its own weight. That is like you rolling a school bus with one hand!

Other bugs are super fast. A cockroach can zoom across a floor in half a second flat. Some bugs can even glow in the dark, like fireflies lighting up a summer night.

A few bugs are incredible jumpers. Fleas can leap over 100 times their own height. The bug world is full of surprises.

BUG BATTLES

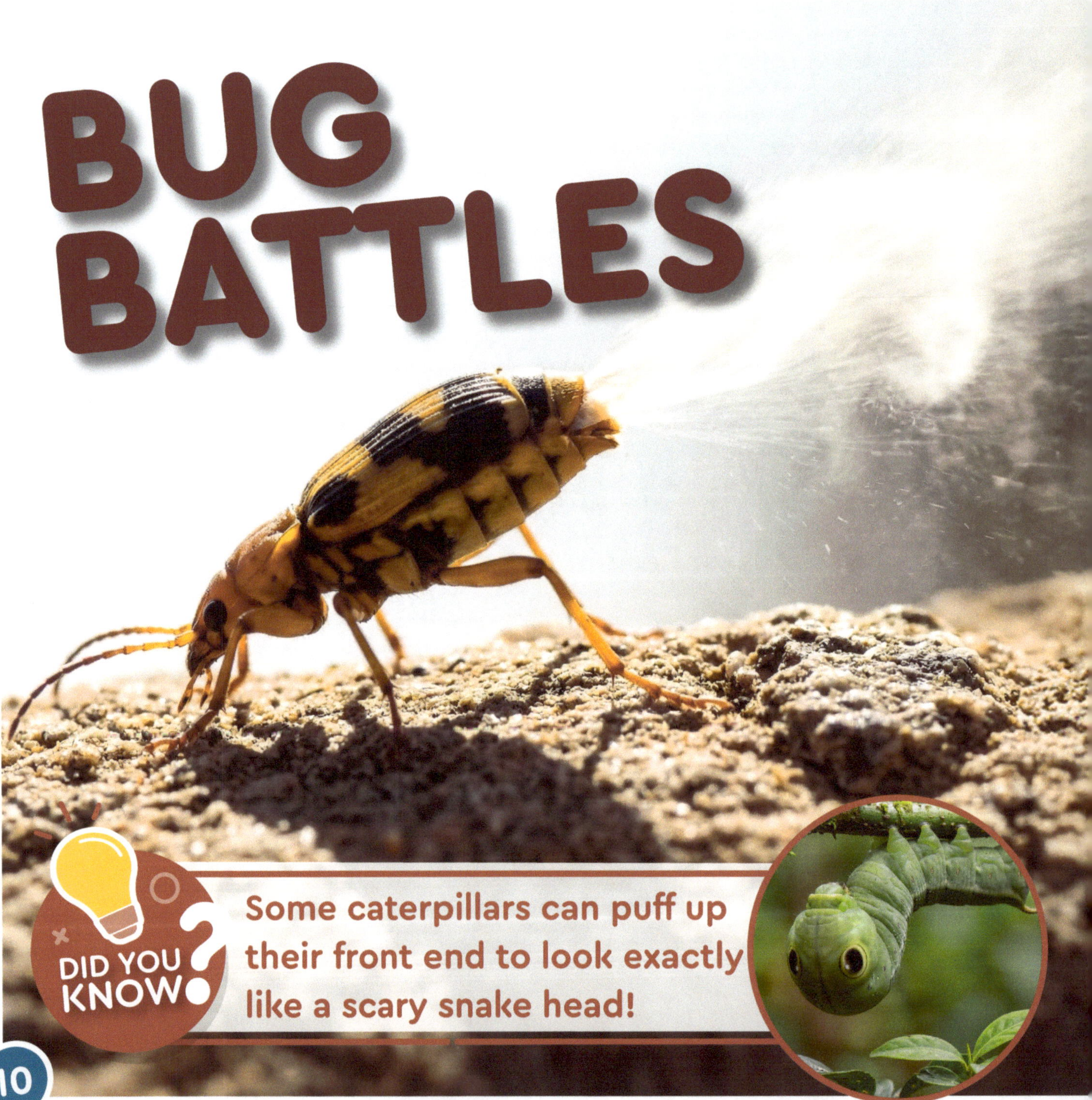

Some caterpillars can puff up their front end to look exactly like a scary snake head!

Hiss! A beetle sprays hot liquid at a hungry spider.

Life is tough for a tiny bug. Some hide by looking like the things around them. Others taste so bad that animals learn to leave them alone.

The bombardier beetle has a wild trick. It shoots boiling hot spray from its body at 212 degrees! This scares away enemies fast.

Some bugs work as a team to stay safe. Ants march in big groups. Bees guard their hive together. In the bug world, staying alive takes hard work and clever tricks.

MANTIS MASTERS

Snap! A praying mantis blends into a branch. It's hungry for lunch!

The praying mantis is a master hunter. It sits perfectly still and waits, its green or brown body blending in with the plants around it. When **prey** comes close, it strikes faster than you can blink!

A mantis has huge eyes that can turn to look around. It is one of the only insects that can look over its own shoulder. Try sneaking up on one. It will turn its head and stare right at you!

Praying mantises live in gardens, forests, and fields all over the world. They eat flies, moths, and even other mantises.

STICK SECRETS

A stick insect can drop a leg to escape a predator, then slowly grow it back over several months.

Crack! What looked like a twig just started to walk away.

Stick insects are the hide-and-seek champs of the bug world. Their long, thin bodies look just like twigs. Birds and lizards walk right past them without a second glance.

These slow-moving bugs mostly come out at night. They munch on leaves in the dark when fewer hunters are searching for a meal.

Stick insects live in forests in warm parts of the world. Some can grow over 2 feet long—as long as your arm! When scared, they freeze perfectly still and wait for danger to pass.

LEAF WALKERS

Rustle! A leaf on the branch starts to move. It's a Walking Leaf!

Walking leaf insects are some of the best hiders in nature. Their flat, green bodies look just like real leaves. They even have lines, spots, and brown edges like a leaf would.

These insects sway gently back and forth as they walk. This makes them look like leaves blowing in the wind. It is a great way to fool hungry birds.

Walking leaf insects live in tropical forests across Asia and Australia. They eat leaves from the same trees where they hide. Talk about living in your food!

TOE-BITER TERROR

Giant water bugs are strong enough to catch and eat frogs, fish, and even small snakes.

Splash! A giant water bug dives down and grabs a small fish.

Giant water bugs are fierce hunters. They live in ponds and streams around the world. These big flat bugs can grow over 4 inches long—longer than your finger! People call them toe-biters because they pinch hard.

A giant water bug hides underwater and waits for food to swim by. Then it grabs its prey with powerful front legs. It uses its sharp beak to inject juices and slurp up its meal.

In some species, the dad carries all the eggs on his back. He keeps them safe until they hatch. What a good father!

ASSASSIN AMBUSH

One sneaky assassin bug stacks dead ant bodies on its back to disguise its smell from living ants.

Thwack! An assassin bug waits for a beetle to walk by. He's hunting!

Assassin bugs are sneaky hunters. There are over 7,000 kinds all over the world. Most have a curved beak that works like a tiny sword.

When an assassin bug finds prey, it jabs its beak in fast. Then it spits special juices that turn the insides into soup. This lets the bug slurp up its meal like a milkshake.

Some assassin bugs hide under bark or inside flowers. They wait patiently for other bugs to wander close. Surprise attacks are their specialty!

TITAN TERROR

Click! A titan beetle's jaws snap shut on a wooden stick.

The titan beetle is one of the biggest bugs on Earth. It can grow over 6 inches long—as long as a grown-up's hand! It lives deep in the rain forests of South America.

Titan beetles have huge jaws that can snap a wooden pencil in half. But they rarely bite people. They use their powerful jaws mostly to scare away enemies.

The wildest thing about titan beetles? Adults never eat. Not once. They spend their short lives looking for a mate, lay their eggs, and then they are gone.

BULLET BITE

DID YOU KNOW?
The burning pain from a single bullet ant sting can last for a full 24 hours without fading.

Zing! A bullet ant squeezes its jaws shut. It's saying "stay back"!

The bullet ant has the most painful sting of any insect on Earth. People say it hurts so much it feels like being shot. That is how it got its name!

Bullet ants live in the rain forests of Central and South America. They build their nests at the base of tall trees. A **colony** can have hundreds of workers, all ready to defend their home.

These fierce ants hunt small bugs and sip sweet tree sap. They march across the forest floor and climb high into the treetops. Most animals, big and small, know better than to mess with a bullet ant.

GEAR GUARDIAN

Chomp! A wheel bug bites down hard on a fly.

The wheel bug has a cool shape on its back. It looks like a tiny gear or cog from a machine! This is the only bug in North America with this strange look.

Wheel bugs move slowly and quietly. They sneak up on other insects without making a sound. Then they jab their sharp beak in and enjoy their meal.

These helpful bugs live in gardens and fields across the eastern United States. They eat pests like stink bugs and caterpillars. Farmers and gardeners are always glad to have them around.

PEANUT PRETENDER

The peanut head bug is also called the alligator bug because its bumpy head looks like a tiny gator snout.

Pop! A strange bug spreads its wings and shows off big eyespots.

The peanut head bug has one of the oddest faces in nature. Its head is shaped like a big unshelled peanut! Scientists think this strange look may scare enemies by making the bug look like a lizard or snake head.

When scared, it opens its wings wide. Bright eyespots flash out suddenly. These spots look like the eyes of a much bigger, scarier animal.

Peanut head bugs live in the rain forests of Central and South America. They are harmless and spend their time quietly sipping tree sap through their long straw-like mouths. All that drama is just for show!

FAKE THORNS

There are over 3,000 species of thorn bugs, and some look like tiny helicopters or horned helmets instead of thorns.

Skritch! A tiny thorn on a branch starts to walk on six legs.

Thorn bugs are tiny trick artists. A tall bump on their back looks just like a sharp thorn. When they sit still on a branch, they blend right in.

These clever bugs often sit in groups on plant stems. A row of thorn bugs looks exactly like a row of real thorns. Birds fly right past without stopping!

Thorn bugs suck sap from plants to eat. They live in warm places around the world. As they drink sap, they make sweet sticky drops called honeydew. Ants love this stuff so much they guard the thorn bugs like bodyguards, keeping enemies away in exchange for a sugary snack!

STRIDER SKATING

Some ocean water striders spend their entire lives on the open sea, hundreds of miles from any shore.

Zip! A water strider glides across the pond without sinking.

Water striders walk on water! Tiny waterproof hairs on their legs trap air bubbles. This keeps them floating on top of the surface like magic. They look like they are skating on glass.

These bugs live on calm ponds, lakes, and slow streams. They feel tiny ripples in the water to find food. When a small bug falls in and struggles, they race over to grab it.

Water striders have six legs, and each pair has a job. The front pair catches food. The middle pair rows like oars. The back pair steers like a rudder.

ZOMBIE SURGEON
DID YOU KNOW?
The jewel wasp stings the exact brain cells that control fear and escape, turning the roach into a willing prisoner.
34

Zzzt! A jewel wasp lands on a cockroach and takes control.

The jewel wasp lives in warm tropical places. Its shiny green and blue body gleams like a precious gem. But this pretty little wasp has a very creepy trick up its wings.

A jewel wasp stings a cockroach in just the right spot in its brain. The sting does not kill it. Instead, the cockroach stops fighting and follows the wasp like a zombie.

The wasp leads the roach to a safe burrow. There it lays an egg on the living cockroach. When the baby wasp hatches, it has fresh food waiting. Gross, but kind of cool!

BUG HEROES

One out of every three bites of food you eat exists because a bee helped pollinate the plant.

Whirr! Bees fly from flower to flower, helping plants grow.

Bugs help people more than you might think. Bees spread **pollen** so plants can make fruits and seeds. Without bees, we would lose apples, almonds, blueberries, and many other favorite foods.

Ladybugs eat pests that harm our crops. Ants dig tunnels that bring fresh air and water into the soil. And silk comes from hardworking silkworms!

Many bugs are in trouble today. Their habitats are shrinking fast. You can help by planting native flowers and keeping your garden safe for these tiny heroes.

BACKYARD WONDERS

Chirp! A cricket sings from a patch of cool, green grass.

You do not need to travel far to find amazing bugs. They are right outside your door! Look under rocks, in tall grass, or near a pond.

Try sitting still and watching closely. You might see an ant carrying a crumb bigger than its own head. Or a butterfly landing softly on a bright flower. You might even spot a lightning bug blinking on and off in your backyard on a warm summer night.

Every bug has a story waiting to be discovered. The more you look, the more you will see. Grab a jar and a notebook, and start your own bug adventure today!

GLOSSARY

thorax
The middle part of an insect's body

prey
An animal that is hunted and eaten by another animal

colony
A group of the same kind of bugs living together

pollen
Tiny powder in flowers that helps plants make seeds

sap
The liquid inside a plant's stems